A SHOUT IN THE STREET

The Story of Church House in Bridgeton

Sally Magnusson

SAINT ANDREW PRESS

EDINBURGH

First published in 1991 on behalf of
CHURCH HOUSE, BRIDGETON
by SAINT ANDREW PRESS
121 George Street, Edinburgh EH2 4YN

ISBN 0 86153 150 7

British Library Cataloguing in Publication Data
Magnusson, Sally
A shout in the street: the story of
Church House in Bridgeton.
I. Title
261. 10941

ISBN 0861531507

Design by Mark Blackadder and Lesley A Taylor.
Printed and bound by McNaughton & Sinclair Ltd, Glasgow.

Dedication

THIS story is dedicated to all those unnamed leaders and helpers who, through fifty years, have created and sustained the life of Church House by their committed enthusiasm and selfless service.

From the dark days of the black-out, through daunting days of difficulty, they have brought warmth and light and love into this House which has been a home for thousands of Bridgeton youngsters. Some of those have found faith; all have found fun and friendship.

Preface

CHURCH House is unique! I know of no other centre like it that has lasted for fifty years and is still going strong, reaching out to young people in need in the name of Christ.

It's a marvellous story and we in Church House are extremely grateful to Sally Magnusson for telling it so well. We hope you will enjoy reading it.

But we hope, also, that this book will challenge others in the Church to think about what they can do to reach out to the young people living around them in the name of Christ. Let's not just leave it up to others. Let us all rise up and build!

HOWARD R HUDSON
Minister of Bridgeton: St Francis-in-the-East
and Chairman of Church House

Contents

'That is God ... a shout in the street'

(James Joyce, *Ulysses*)

IT'S easier to get into the Kingdom of Heaven, so they say, than into Church House in the heart of Glasgow's East End.

For fifty years, successive generations of Bridgeton's more inventive young minds have been devising methods of illegal entry. Tunnelling was even tried at one time, until one enterprising invader popped his head up through the floor of the gym and had it kicked in. Descent through the roof has proved a popular alternative.

So it's no wonder that when the battered steel door of Church House swings open, you feel as if you're entering a fortification. As the current leader, Alex Mair, puts it, 'We know our kids. Everything that moves here, disappears.'

You walk past the caged gym, the grim concrete walls, the bolted-down tables and chairs of the canteen. Then round the corner of the gym and a big painted sign greets you: The Upper Room. Inside is a tiny chapel, two benches down each side and a table in the middle, a piece of stained glass in the wall presiding like an altar-piece. Glass? Real, breakable, beautiful glass in this building? Yes, and un-vandalized hymn-books and an air of musty reverence that speaks unmistakably of worship.

What is this place, this bizarre mixture of church and fortress? How on earth does a building which has clearly had a few worldly experiences in its time manage to evoke this sense of jaunty holiness?

And how, you can only wonder as you look round the wasted landscape of modern Bridgeton, has this funny old relic survived at all?

Church House is a story of survival. When it came into being in 1942, it was against the odds, and it's been fighting those odds ever since. It was here, one August evening in the middle of the Second World War, that a man called Arthur Gray asked eleven boys to meet him in a near-derelict church building in Boden Street, in the heart of Glasgow's East End. Among the dirt, dust and broken windows, they found an old joiner's bench. And there, by the light of two candles, they read the story of Nehemiah, the humble servant who was called to build up the ruined city of Jerusalem. 'Let us rise up and build' was to be their challenge too.

Jerusalem, with its broken walls and its gates consumed by fire, can scarcely have seemed a more daunting task to the Rev Arthur Gray than the job before him in Boden Street. He was out to rebuild more than the fabric of a neglected church; his call was to rebuild lives.

CHURCH HOUSE,
BRIDGETON

The Pals

ARTHUR Gray was the minister of St Francis-in-the-East, a few blocks away in Queen Mary Street, a church which had itself risen almost miraculously from the ashes of a dying parish. Gray inherited the charge from the Rev Sydney Warnes, who is the first in a remarkable line of immense, visionary characters to inhabit the Bridgeton story. Warnes came to Bridgeton in 1930 for the simple reason that no-one else would take the charge.

The church, at that time called Barrowfield Church, was about to be closed down. It had lost touch with the people; the congregation had dwindled to fewer than thirty; even the gas and water had been cut off. Inevitably, Glasgow Presbytery moved that the charge be suppressed, but Sidney Warnes—at that time comfortably installed in St Mary's, Partick—argued powerfully that the Church had to have a presence in an area like Bridgeton. 'To take down the flag in a place where thousands are in urgent need of the ministrations of the Church would be tragic for the Church,' he insisted.

His passion carried the day, and the Home Board of the Kirk offered to provide a stipend. But no-one was willing to take on a job of such awesome magnitude and uncertain prospects. In the end Sydney Warnes volunteered himself. A few hours before his induction in January 1930, the plaster of the vestry ceiling fell in.

Warnes was soon a well-kent figure in Bridgeton, and it did not take him long to build up the church organisation. He was a remarkable man. Brought up in an

REV
SYDNEY H R WARNES

3

orphan home, he had been a music hall pianist before entering the ministry—a skill that would stand him in good stead in his new charge. Sociable and determined, with an unmistakable twinkle in his eye, he had the priceless gift of being able to generate enthusiasm and win loyalty. People loved him.

He soon had volunteers scrubbing out the building and lapsed members back in their pews. But that wasn't enough for Sydney Warnes. He only needed to step into the streets to see that Bridgeton in the 1930s required more of its church than a full Sunday programme.

The Depression had a grip on the whole community. Unemployed men hung aimlessly around the street corners, the younger ones drifted into gangs and conflict was endemic. It was a problem that received dramatic publicity when Lord Alness, in giving judgement in the High Court on a crime of violence, focussed the attention of the whole city on the condition of its youth. Sydney Warnes felt the challenge personally. What should the Church be doing? What should he be doing?

His first answer was to approach the unemployed lads on the street corner and organise a football match. Next, he invited them to the tiny hall at the back of the church to form a club, which they decided to call the Pals'

Club. The place was packed every available night, but the accommodation was hopelessly inadequate and there was no room for extension of the premises.

One day, standing in the empty church which was so much useless space for six days of the week, Sydney Warnes had a vision of that space dedicated to a new usefulness—a vision which was later to become a pattern for many churches in a similar predicament. By determined, dynamic drive, he roused the enthusiasm of others and raised the princely sum of £2,200 to transform the interior of the church.

The galleries were taken down and a new floor stretched across the church at that level. The upper storey became a simple sanctuary which could still seat five hundred people, and the space on the ground floor provided a large hall, a billiard room and a reading room. Even the basement was refashioned, with a new boiler-house, to provide the luxury of baths at a nominal price. By the end of 1930, the transformation was complete.

The church even got a new name to symbolise its fresh identity. St Francis-in-the-East, they called it, and it became a focus for Christian brotherliness towards the unemployed in the city. The Pals' Club grew to a membership of nearly five hundred, and for 1d a week

'PAL' WARNES AT THE PIANO

Of course, life among the Pals was no picnic, and many a time members had to be quietly divested of weaponry more lethal than a boxing glove before they could be admitted. But Sydney Warnes seems to have had the effortless knack of winning their respect. He entertained them at the piano and beat them at billiards and handed out packets of Woodbine when they put in a good evening's work at reclaiming the football pitch.

There are stories, recorded in John Sim's excellent booklet, *A Light in Bridgeton*, of Warnes' almost legendary generosity and dedication to the people he served. He used to run a soup kitchen at 1d a pint. He organised the distribution of sacks of potatoes to the most needy. He ladled free herring from trucks at the railway yard into whatever receptacle came to hand; even, apparently, pillow-slips.

It's hardly surprising that he made himself ill in the end, and by 1934, with a congregation swollen from thirty to three hundred, and the church's commitment to the community established, he knew it was time to go; that August he was called to Buckie in the north-east of Scotland. But who on earth could follow Sydney Warnes? Or, as the elder of a neighbouring church put it, less charitably, 'You'll never get another man for that place.'

subscription you could be there every night, making furniture in the joinery class, treading the boards in the drama club, practising your right hook on boxing night, or honing your skills on the full-sized billiard table donated by a regimental club in Glasgow. Later the youths got the use of a patch of waste ground for a football pitch.

Enter the Rev Arthur Gray. He was a young man, lean and energetic, and this was his first charge. By the time he arrived at St Francis-in-the-East, it had been vacant for almost a year and had lost much of the impetus that Sydney Warnes had invested. The Pals' Club especially had dwindled, partly in the absence of its charismatic founder, but also because various uniformed church organisations had started to meet on the premises and the Pals were now confined to the billiard room. Arthur Gray was keenly aware of how pathetically inadequate the facilities were. Billiards and dominoes were better than nothing, but for men suffering the full awfulness of the Depression, he felt he had precious little to offer.

Gray has left a graphic account of what life was like for Bridgeton folk in those years, the years leading up to the founding of Church House. He wrote:

'The Depression meant women standing at each close mouth and groups of men at each street corner. It meant rationing by money (heel-pads for dinner and a piece-in-dip—on the good days). It meant men idle for anything up to twelve years if they were unskilled. It meant for them the loss of confidence, fear that someone would speak for them and they would let them down if they were to get a job. It meant drift.

'Men used to go out to a wee hut one of them had near East Kilbride or in that direction. They'd leave Bridgeton about 11 am and walk out and roast potatoes there. They used to talk for hours on this kind of question: "How can you get from Glasgow Cross to Cambuslang without going under a bridge?" Then home about 7 am the next morning and into bed. The seasons or the day or night came to mean nothing.

'Clyde Football Club used to open their ground one morning a week to let "the unemployed" watch the practice game. And about 8,000 and upwards gathered. Among them the best hands on the Clyde and men who later marched from El Alamein to Berlin.

'We've never come to terms with unemployment; have thought that once men were working, it was all over and

REV
ARTHUR H GRAY

6

done with. But how deep the scars have gone. I knew a boy who was 12 years of age before he saw his father go out to work. And there were hundreds like him, and thousands if you reduce the figure 12 to ten, or eight, or six. The amount of industrial quiet there has been since the War is a permanent amazement to me and the best tribute to the character of working men who lived through what I've hinted at.'

Arthur Gray was deeply, passionately moved by the conditions around him. Like Sydney Warnes, he was able, by dint of visiting the homes in the parish, working at friendships and inspiring the various church groups, to build up the congregation again slowly. But he was always aware of the thousands of homes untouched either by the Church or by that Christian hope that could make a difference to hopeless, drifting lives. He just didn't know how to get to them.

Practically, he did what he could. About 1938, he became friendly with a works manager of a new concern in Scotland who, whenever he needed men, would get in touch. Once the word got round that the St Francis minister had access to jobs, he was besieged. Twice a week he interviewed men in the vestry, listening to the heart-breaking 'special reasons' why each man felt he ought to

be chosen. In the end, there were more than 400 names on his list, and about 120 got work before the war came.

'That kind of interviewing and listening to these stories broke me in a way that the normal job didn't,' Arthur Gray commented later. By 1939, he had reached the point, indeed, where he felt that he had achieved all he could at Bridgeton and ought to move on. Only 'prevenient grace' stopped him at that time, he said— 'a peculiar hunch that was far deeper than reason which kept me where I was.'

It was that *coup de grâce* that saved Arthur Gray for one of the most imaginative and ultimately long-lasting inner-city youth ventures in the history of the Church of Scotland.

He also received crucial encouragement at the time from the newly fledged Iona Community, founded the previous year by the Rev George MacLeod (latterly the Very Rev Lord MacLeod of Fuinary). He had resigned from his parish of Govan Old, over the river from Bridgeton, because of his experiences in the mid-thirties Depression. With most of his parishioners unemployed, MacLeod saw then that the Church had lost the allegiance of masses of the working class. He believed it had failed them.

In the Pearce Institute he had done the same as Sydney Warnes and had vastly greater resources than Arthur Gray, but he knew that Scotland and its Church needed more. His vision was to weld the working class and the Church into a new community for Scotland. The vision took practical form in creating a community of skilled artisans and apprentice ministers to rebuild the ruined living quarters in the precincts of Iona Abbey. In the winter, the Church probationers worked in teams in inner city, industrial and new housing areas around the country.

George MacLeod was passionately convinced that only by experiments in new ways of life and work could the Church make the faith live for workers in the new industrial age. Arthur Gray grasped that vision like a drowning man. In the Iona Community's analysis he found accurately described the conditions with which he was wrestling in Bridgeton. And it gave him the confidence to pursue an idea that had been quietly incubating in his mind for years.

The Pals' Club was the clue. Slowly it had begun to dawn on him that this was like a seed, 'tiny yet vital, and with possibilities of growth in it.' Even if it was just billiards and dominoes, men, he realised, became a group as they shared the secular interests of recreation, a group aware of itself with growing friendships, a fellowship through which some of them began to find a faith. On a Thursday night, some of the Pals used to join a few church members for what the minister called simple family prayers. It was an occasion which, as he put it in his understated way, 'I think, meant something.'

He explained the basis of his thinking some years later to a reporter of the *Scottish Daily Mail*. In words that sound uncannily apposite today, he said:

'There is a colossal gap between the Church and young people—and not only young people. And if people are to understand the Church, it must be done through an experience and not just through teaching in the old sense.

'Moody and Sankey could produce the response they did because people had a common Christian background. Certain truths were accepted. That isn't so now. So we have to produce the response and provide the background at the same time. We try to do that by fellowship.

'Christ came into the world in a body. Therefore the ordinary bodily things of the world have a dignity which should be respected. Fellowship is a good thing— even the ordinary fellowship which exists in a group of men round a billiard table.'

The genesis of what was later to be Church House came in the realisation that what was needed was the Pals' Club on a bigger scale. This was Arthur Gray's vision:

'The getting of a place which would be to those who came to it the centre for interests which they liked, and would be for those of us running it the expression of the Church in everyday life. The bread and wine from the Table being in another shape and form, but being shared just the same. And to have in it something like the Thursday night family prayers we had grown used to.'

With that idea before him, Gray began a long and wearying hunt for premises. As early as 1937, when the thought first began to germinate, he had approached the Home Board of the Church of Scotland for financial assistance. The Board said they would pay, but year after year passed without a suitable site becoming available, and Gray really did begin to think he had reached the end of the road. The only piece of vacant ground was in Walkinshaw Street, beside Anderson's mill. But permission to build there was refused because the ground, they were told, was needed for future development. It was later sold to the Corporation to build a sub-police station.

Gray was then offered the staggering sum of £1,000 as a gift from the Union of Boys Clubs if he could only

find the right place, but again he was stymied at every turn. The money eventually went elsewhere.

Then the elderly minister of the neighbouring church, London Road East, offered a union, in which his church would be converted into a centre for the new work. Hopes rose again at St Francis. But the other Kirk Session flatly rejected the idea.

It was a further two years before the answer came. During that time the Second World War sucked most of the men to the Forces and the Pals' Club was no more, but Arthur Gray's vision persisted. Yes, the men were gone, but something, he felt, could still be done for the young people, left largely to their own devices on the streets now that their fathers were away and their mothers, often employed on war work, were bearing the strain of the household alone. Something could be made, too, for the men to come back to when the war was done.

Then at last it happened. The neighbouring minister resigned, and the eleven members who turned up at the final meeting decided to convey the buildings to the Home Board and dissolve the congregation. The two parishes were joined. The Home Board stood by their old commitment to St Francis-in-the-East, and agreed to pay both the cost of renovating the church building and the salaries of two club leaders for five years.

Arthur Gray was profoundly grateful: 'I have never since ceased to admire the Home Board for that courageous act in the midst of war,' he records, 'and when they had no obligation of any kind to act in such a changed situation.'

The cost of transforming London Road East Church into what was officially described as 'a community centre for the youth of the district', was estimated at £1,100. In fact, the final cost was £1,300. The workmen moved in, and it was there, in August 1942, amid the debris of the building work, that Arthur Gray held his first club meeting.

Church House was on its way.

Desecrated to the Glory of God

IT was a huge building, with seating for fourteen hundred people. But the dust of eight months lay on it, blown through windows long broken. The workmen had added to the chaos by ripping the long semi-circular pews from the floor and flinging them one on top of the other. There was no electric light, only dirt and decay and ruin.

That late August evening, Arthur Gray and his little band gathered below the gallery. The eleven teenagers stood with the leaders, Norman Hutchison and Jim Chisholm, in a half-circle between two pillars, while the minister walked over to stand beneath a broken window, through which the night sky glimmered. The workmen had left behind a tiny carpenter's bench and two candles were placed there, the same candles which for years to come would flicker in front of an ever-larger body of watchers at the annual rededication service, until at last their light was spent.

In an article which he wrote for a youth magazine in 1947, Arthur Gray described that first wartime service:

'A word was spoken about our ruined surroundings; a reminder was given of Allan Street not far off where a land-mine had fallen on tenement houses; a sentence about Rotterdam, Warsaw and other blitzed cities.

'Then some verses of Nehemiah chapter two, towards the end of the chapter—of another company amid other ruins, and the challenge and call from these ruins through which God spoke and people answered, "Let us rise up and build". A prayer, the Lord's Prayer, the Blessing. And a new club was born.'

In the weeks to come, the renovation was completed. The church was cleared of pews and pulpit, and the wood used to provide partitions to make small rooms under the gallery, separate boys' and girls' games rooms, a canteen and a chapel. The colour scheme was pale blue and primrose. The gallery remained empty—'a perpetual challenge to further extension,' as Arthur Gray put it. The large hall became a gym, a dance hall and an auditorium for club shows. The smaller hall served as a library and a place to gather on Sunday evenings.

Never, joked one visitor whom Arthur Gray took round the building, had he seen a church 'so desecrated to the glory of God.' It is a remark which Arthur Gray's successors, empty-pursed guardians of Church House against the depredations of time and the vandals, have had occasion to repeat wryly down the years.

The eleven boys soon brought along others and the club began to thrive. The next task was to get the girls along. Gray contacted as many in the parish as he could think of and asked them to come along to Boden Street with a friend. On a cold, foggy November night, he sat them down for a chat. This was a new experience for the Bridgeton lassies, who sat and gazed at the minister in awestruck silence. It was one Ruby Woodburn who saved the hour. Just as the young minister was beginning to get hot under the collar, she piped up, 'Mister, can we come and scrub the flair?'

The next Thursday, senior boys and girls met officially for the first time—in dungarees and overalls and armed with pails and brushes. One boy at least loudly gave thanks for the blackout that hid his pail from jeering comments at the street corners as he passed. Thus was inaugurated what became the annual ritual of club cleaning. The floors were scrubbed, the woodwork washed, all crockery and cutlery specially cleaned. It became a great and joyous carry-on, involving much throwing of wet cloths, and was for a long time considered one of the best nights of the club year.

So that was the girls in, too. That Christmas they all had their first dance, with a tree and a real sense of belonging. The building was dedicated by George MacLeod, leader of the Iona Community, who had been so consistently supportive of the work in Bridgeton. He went round Church House with the youngsters in his wake, opening each door and asking a blessing. Later, the building was officially opened, in the presence of the Lord Provost of Glasgow, by the Very Rev Dr John White, the presbytery leader who had supported Sydney Warnes' plea to keep Barrowfield Parish Church open.

One of the girls from that time remembers the heady excitement of those early days. Grace Donald had received a letter from the minister saying he was starting a youth club and would she like to come. She did.

'We drew up a syllabus,' she says, 'helped by the wonderful leaders Mr Gray brought. They were all professional people. To us, living in the old, grey tenements, with toilets out on the landing, this was a different world.

We arranged discussion groups, cookery, sewing, drama, badminton, basketball, indoor football, musical evenings, a party booking for the Alhambra Theatre. To me, this was wonderful. I shall never forget what Church House, Mr Gray and his friends did for us, giving up all their spare time for us.

'Each night we had our canteen, all taking turns to serve spam, dried egg, whatever rations would allow. Our evenings finished with prayers in our small chapel. Each fortnight we had a dance, a lady from the church playing the piano. Again Mr Gray and his leaders all came—and remember, this was during the black-out.'

As time went on and the numbers grew, the club was divided into sections—junior, intermediate and senior for both sexes. The leaders had meant to concentrate on the 14 to 18 age-group, where they perceived the greatest need. But as Arthur Gray said, 'We found that if the Church's biggest job is to express fellowship so that folk can find a faith, then it isn't possible to limit that principle to one age group.'

So there came into being eighter and tenner groups for the younger brothers and sisters, and eventually a twenties section and a men's group. Five years after those first eleven boys enrolled in the darkness, the club had swollen to almost five hundred boys, girls and men.

Arthur Gray's great talent was to attract and enthuse a band of indefatigable voluntary leaders. From that day to this, the volunteers have been the backbone of Church House, the teamwork between them and the paid leaders has been the catalyst of its success: men and women who down the years have given up their evenings to travel to the club from various parts of the city, to 'do their bit' for the youngsters and enjoy the fellowship created in that place by men like Arthur Gray and his successors.

Helpers were often enlisted from the ranks of the university students in the city. One of the two first salaried youth leaders, Jim Chisholm, paid his way through college by helping Arthur Gray establish the club. He brought along a divinity student from Glasgow University called John Sim, who had been invalided out of the air force. Sim spent his spare evenings at Church House as a volunteer, little imagining then that he would be running the place himself before too many years had passed. Church House has a habit of getting hold of you that way.

These helpers did a tremendous job in inspiring the youngsters they worked with. One teenager in the intermediate section was a lad called Jim Herd who worked with John Sim on a club newspaper, showing such promise that, when he left school, Jim Chisholm got him a job on *The Glasgow Herald* as a copy boy. He went on to become a greatly respected journalist in both newspapers and broadcasting, and never forgot what he owed to Church House.

As James Herd recalled himself once in an article, from the night in 1942 when one of the leaders clambered over the debris to ask for his name and address and enrolled him as a member of the juniors, to the time he left *The Scotsman* to look after itself while he dashed off to Helenvale Park to run for Church House in the inter-club sports, the club in Boden Street remained a lynchpin in his life. Later, like so many of the youngsters who 'found themselves' at Church House, he became a dedicated volunteer and an elder in St Francis-in-the-East itself. Many years after, while speaking at the rededication of a rebuilt Church House in 1974, he collapsed with a brain haemorrhage from which he sadly never recovered.

The helpers who had such a profound influence on boys like Jim Herd in the early days were assiduously collected by Arthur Gray, who never let an opportunity of enlisting a volunteer slip by. One Monday morning in 1942, a young teacher called David Gray boarded a

Number 9 Auchenshuggle tram in the West End of Glasgow and headed east to start a new career in Bernard Street Junior Secondary School. But as it turned out, his real career in Bridgeton would develop not in the school, but a hundred yards away in Boden Street.

Leaving the school one evening, he noticed a van parked outside a dilapidated old church and joiners carrying wood down a lane. After negotiating his way past the puddles in the lane, he struck up conversation with the minister of St Francis and expressed an interest in the new youth club. That was it. David Gray was in and, for many years after, he used to go straight from school to Church House every evening and with great difficulty make the last tram at Bridgeton Cross for Hillhead.

He was soon mucking in with the two full time boys' leaders, Jim Chisholm, the artistic college boy, and Norman Hutchison, a doctor's son who liked the outdoor, practical life and shared with David Gray a passion for spaghetti, which they tucked into together on the nights that David missed the last tram home.

Right from the start the trips outside the club, away from Bridgeton, were among the most popular pursuits, and remain so to this day. In the early days of Church House, there was a weekend camp at Hut Point in

Braidwood in Lanarkshire, which had been erected through the good offices of the parish minister, the Rev George Candlish. The leaders used to take groups of boys and girls in an SMT bus from Waterloo Street. David Gray, well used to the comforts of his West End home, was always slightly puzzled by the popularity of Hut Point, with its extremely basic amenities: an earth cludgie (toilet), ablutions in the burn and cooking on a Victorian open fire, supplemented by primus stoves which seldom worked. They slept in the main hut with leaders' room attached and an annexe known as 'The Dunny'. It was very cold.

But for youngsters who in all their lives had known only the bleak and often squalid realities of Bridgeton, it was heaven. As Grace Donald remembers:

'Those weekends were the highlight for us. Mr Cunningham, the farmer, gave us barns. There was a stream running through the land where we washed, peeled potatoes, did the dishes. Oh, the fun we had getting away from the city.'

Back at Church House, the numbers and activities continued to expand. The report for 1943-44 has a programme of bewildering variety—including country dancing, handicrafts, art, netball, table-tennis, club newspaper, woodwork, decoration, visiting speaker, books, leathercraft, a 'men only' discussion group, billiards, debates, health and homecraft, drama, film group,

'HUT POINT'

men would return from the Forces. And perhaps most encouraging of all, the older boys and girls were beginning to help out with the younger sections, run the canteen and assist in the Sunday Schools. 'In the long run,' said Arthur Gray in his report, 'the acceptance of individual responsibility is the one mark of growth that matters.'

In his remaining years at Church House, Arthur Gray—now officially designated 'chairman'—continued to be the heart and soul of the place. He and his assistants were the bridge between the club and the church down the road. He knew everyone, knew how to talk to them and share their interests, their hopes, and their problems. And he knew how to laugh. His ardent devotion to Glasgow Rangers made for many a tease and many an impassioned debate on a Saturday evening.

What everyone says about Arthur Gray is that he knew the guidance of the Spirit. He walked closely with his God and the people around him felt it. 'In Arthur Gray we all met Jesus Himself,' it was said of him many years later. At Church House he imparted an awareness

football training, poster drawing, badminton and a class beguilingly dubbed 'electricity'.

Football matches were organised and a pantomime produced. Members from all sections had a weekly swim at Shettleston Baths. The new men's group was the beginning of a move to reflect a wider family life, also helping to keep the door open against the day when the

18

of the Christian faith to youngsters who hardly noticed it was happening. That unexpected fragrance of holiness which is about Church House still, emanated in the first instance from Arthur Gray.

He it was who instigated the practice of closing each evening with short prayers in the chapel, which club members themselves had reclaimed from the debris. They stained the floor of the sanctuary and installed concealed lighting. With the first gift of money the club ever received, they bought material—'green as the countryside in Spring,' said Arthur Gray—and the girls made it into curtains to hang in front of the boarded-up windows. Two boys constructed a Table from broken pews and one of them made a simple Cross to stand in front of the curtains. Gathered there in the chapel, leaders and members would bring the day to a close.

David Gray commented later: 'A great tribute to Arthur was his skill in persuading leaders to take prayers, and I marvelled at seeing quite inarticulate souls bravely standing behind the Communion Table.

'Following a hectic tenners' Christmas party, Arthur led a very perspiring band into the chapel and asked, "What shall we thank God for?" A wee chap piped up,

THE CHURCH HOUSE CHAPEL

"Thank God for fun!" Surely he had captured the essence of his club.'

Surely he had. As had the boys' leader, Norman Hutchison, when the leaders emerged from the chapel one evening after a long meeting. 'The fellowship of the Holy Spirit!' he said to Arthur Gray, 'I never knew what that meant till I came here.'

Every Sunday night they stood in the chapel, members and leaders, and spoke the words that kept the club's beginnings always in mind. The responses were always the same:

Leader: Except the Lord build the house

Members: They labour in vain that build it.

Leader: Except the Lord keep the city

Members: The watchman waketh but in vain.

Leader: Come let us build up the walls of Jerusalem.

Members: Let us rise up and build.

For Arthur Gray, the regular repetition of these responses was vital, as a reminder of the time 'when the few who have now become so many first heard God speak through our ruins, that in this East End of Glasgow new things might be begun.'

For many of those who practically lived in Church House, those Sunday nights were the best times of all. When the programme for the evening was over, the leaders and the older members would clatter into the canteen, like a family gathering in the kitchen. David Gray remembered that 'despite a heavy day, Arthur always

finished up at the club to say goodnight to Beanie and to Jim Craig's granny' (whoever they might have been).

Then the chairman took off his jacket and dried the dishes. That done, he seems to have had an uncanny knack of sensing unhappiness or uneasiness around him and, instead of slipping off home, could usually be found whiling away the evening in a corner with a member or a leader, unravelling the problem.

By 1950, though, he felt it was time to move on. The foundations had been laid, Church House was thriving and the next chapter belonged to someone else. Arthur Gray knew how much still had to be done. He had already drawn the attention of the Home Board to the need for an extension to the building, a floor to the gallery, for instance, to accommodate the growing numbers and range of activities. And in that same 1947 memorandum, he had argued passionately for the continuation of the club.

'The work at Church House,' he wrote then, 'attempts to express in method and spirit the approach to young people most commended by Church youth workers in this and other lands. These can be summed up thus: going where the people are, beginning at the point people are, and through fellowship to faith.'

They had already seen the fruits of this approach at Church House, he said. It was now established as a real place in the parish, with strong links to the parish church. At a time when the background to the lives of present and future members was growing more unstable, 'the need that gave rise to the birth of Church House exists still to plead for the club's continued life,' he wrote.

His plea was answered, but it was left to another to take the club forward into the fifties. During the seven-month vacancy after Arthur Gray departed for North Church, Aberdeen, his namesake 'Uncle David' Gray, as he was known to all, held the reins. The following February, 1951, the new man arrived.

The Rev John Sim entered the fray.

How long is Love patient?

OF course, the man who became minister of St Francis-in-the-East and chairman of Church House in 1951 was really no stranger to the place. John Sim felt as if he were coming home. Seven years previously, when the club was still heady and new, he had travelled across the city in his student days to play his part as a voluntary leader. It was an experience which had helped prepare him for the job he was doing later when the call came to Bridgeton—that of warden of the Barony Kirkhouse Youth Community.

The Barony Kirkhouse was an Iona Trust outreach project in association with The Barony of Glasgow. Norman MacLeod, grandfather of George, had been minister of The Barony in the mid-1800s and had built the 'Moleskin Kirk' in a poor corner of his parish for the working folk of Parliamentary Road. George MacLeod's Iona Youth Trust revitalised the old church after Sydney Warnes had shown the way.

So John Sim took with him to Bridgeton a wealth of experience of city youngsters. His new wife, Jean, who had been the girls' leader at Barony Kirkhouse, was also well prepared for the demands of their new parish.

But it was not only John Sim's experience of youth work that made him an ideal successor to Arthur Gray. Perhaps more importantly, he was, like Gray, an 'Iona man'. The Iona Community's support, both practical and philosophical, continued to underpin the work of Church House. John Sim, like his predecessor (and indeed his successor, Bill Shackleton) was imbued with its ideals. He believed passionately in sustaining the eroding witness of the Church in ravaged communities like Bridgeton.

REV JOHN SIM
WITH CHURCH HOUSE FRIEND
JOSEPH KWASHI

Arthur Gray was inevitably a hard act to follow. But Sim was relieved to find that his ghost did not hover forlornly about the place. In fact, Church House felt the same as ever, the fellowship still vital, the welcome warm. 'Like all true builders of the spirit,' he wrote in his first annual report, 'Arthur Gray left behind him the great values which he himself had sustained.'

Sim's great gift was as an organiser. He was formidably energetic, and tackled the running of Church House with vigour, building up the links between Boden Street and the church in Queen Mary Street, and in the early fifties virtually acting as warden. He still remembers painting scenery for the Christmas pantomime on the afternoon of its opening, with an electric fire in one hand and paintbrush in the other.

Sim found Church House at that time to be one of the most impressive clubs in Glasgow. Since it had established itself with youngsters from the church and their friends, others wanting to be part of it had to conform to decent standards of behaviour. His experience at Barony Kirkhouse had taught him the cardinal rule of running a youth club: you must decide the clientele of the club and stick to it. If the leaders don't, the members will decide things for you. The more disciplined will leave if the less disciplined are not firmly dealt with. If a club gets a reputation for trouble, parents exert their authority and forbid their children to frequent it.

Temporary suspension proved an effective sanction. In an area where there was so little to occupy the idle time of the children of these teeming tenements, Church House was popular. On a vestry night at the church, the minister would get banned teenagers begging him to intercede with the leaders who had exercised that last sanction and shut the door on them.

But as Sim says: 'The club was by no means full of plaster saints, who would soon have had their arms, and heads, chopped off. Bridgeton, scene of big gang warfare in the depression years of the thirties, bred its youngsters tough and streetwise, but many of the single ends and rooms and kitchens were little palaces inside, although the stairheads were crumbling and smelly with common lavatories. In these homes standards were firm and, in almost every home in the area, the church and its representatives were accepted as an important aspect of the local community.'

When Sim started a Friends of Church House movement, he produced a confidential pamphlet, offering interested supporters pen portraits of some of the

teenagers in the club. Here is how he described 17-year-old Johnny, whose family were often in trouble with the police and had recently been charged, all of them, with breach of the peace, after a stairhead fracas.

'This summer,' Sim reported, 'as one of the leaders of a local gang, Johnny was involved in a gang fight. He was brandishing an axe when someone shouted that the police were coming. Johnny's mother, who was standing watching in a close-mouth, called to him: "Here, son, gie us yer axe." After the police had passed, she returned it to him. One of the neighbours remonstrated with her: "Whit did ye do that fur?" "Oh, well," she replied, "the laddie has to defend himsel' somehow."'

Sim went on: 'Johnny has only been a club member for about a year. He has a vicious temper which he tries desperately hard to control, but he has been given no moral standards to help him. It can be justifiably claimed that Johnny's one great chance of becoming a responsible adult is if he stays in the club for the next few years. There, only, is he likely to learn how to control himself by accepting, perhaps unconsciously, basic moral standards.'

Sim also described young Bobby who, at the age of nine, had lived alone with his seven-year-old brother in a single-end for the entire length of the war, when his widowed father was called up. A neighbour had kept them fed and sent them to school. Bobby joined the club at 11 and, by 16, his name was a byword for trouble. Always fighting, always being suspended and coming back for more.

But the club was virtually his home and gradually its standards began to infiltrate. By the age of 23, he was a church member and chairman of the local Christian Workers' League. One former leader, who had known Bobby in his wildest days, walked into the church one night and saw him leading a Bible study. 'He's still recovering from the shock,' Sim reported.

In 1955 St Francis-in-the-East reached its silver jubilee and the artist, Walter Pritchard, painted a striking mural behind the Communion Table of St Francis restoring the ruined church of St Damian. Sydney Warnes and Arthur Gray, who were invited back for the celebrations, must have felt that much of their work of restoring the church to the heart of the Bridgeton community was coming to fruition.

There were now over 700 communicant members with 330 children in the Sunday Schools. There were 300 in the various youth sections of Church House, as well as 50 in the recently started old folks' club. The ties between Queen Mary Street and Boden Street were strong and interwoven. Young adults from Church House had formed a Bible study group at the church and action arising out of study had involved the group in work on behalf of tuberculosis patients, bed-ridden sick, a children's home, political parties and trades unions. Most of the group had become church members. The Iona ideals were taking root.

The rapport between club and church had its piquant moments. One of John Sim's fondest memories is of the evening in Holy Week when club members walked to the church to join the service. 'This was the accepted pattern,' he says, 'although at times there were those who got lost along the way.

'I vividly remember being in the middle of the opening prayer when a tremendous battering on the front door reverberated throughout the building. No-one moved. The banging and the prayer went on, until a raucous voice penetrated the sanctuary: "If ye don't open this bloody door, we'll kick it in." Somebody obliged and several tough teens quietly entered and sidled into a back pew.'

How to deal with their more rumbustious clientele proved then, and has since, a perennial problem for Church House. In the fifties, the gang spirit was still prevalent. But although knives and razors came out on occasions, these were not really the vicious fighting gangs of the thirties. What caused the club leadership the greatest heart-searching was the discontent and the instinctive aggressiveness that some of the boys displayed. No-one outside the club appeared to have the slightest interest in them and they were often in and out of prison. But inside the club they were causing disturbances and infecting others.

John Sim wrote at that time of the 'searching questions' that were arising at Church House. 'How long,' he asked, 'is love very patient, very kind? How often do you forgive? Is it more important that a boy with all the makings of a criminal career before him should learn that if he misbehaves he will be expelled, or that for the first time in his life he knows what it is to be forgiven and trusted?'

Those questions were brought into sharp focus in 1955 when a young man called Geoff Shaw arrived at Church House as club leader. Ronnie Giles and Tom Wright had held the fort during the early fifties, powerfully supported by Monica Morris, who was in charge of the girls' work. Monica, daughter of the St Enoch Hogganfield manse, was a tall, handsome blonde who could handle the boys as effectively as the girls, and there came a period when she carried the whole responsibility while John Sim looked fruitlessly for a boys' leader with the calibre to carry on the work.

Geoff Shaw, who was later to become one of the most charismatic political leaders in Scotland before his untimely death at the age of 51, was trying at that time to set up a team ministry in the Gorbals. After a comfortable Edinburgh upbringing and with the promise of a brilliant academic career before him, Shaw had decided to devote his life to the poor and the outcasts of society. Profoundly influenced by a period working in the immigrant ghettos of East Harlem in New York, he and two other ministers wanted to build a Christian community in the Gorbals—at that time one of the worst slums in Europe. When Glasgow Presbytery turned down their first application, they looked for other work in the area to establish their credentials.

When Geoff Shaw turned up at Church House, he seemed to Sim the ideal solution to their crying need for a club leader. Years of youth work had given him all the qualifications, and more. But Sim was uneasy. Shaw made it clear in their conversations that, if he came to Church House, it would be to specialise in 'the lowest ten

per cent'. In other words, no suspensions: even for a month.

This was all very well. Sim understood and respected Shaw's determination to identify with those at the bottom of the pile. But he had been down this road before in his previous job as warden of the Barony Kirkhouse. By taking in gang types to try to help them, the club itself had become embroiled in gang warfare. Sim had had to watch the 'decent kids' disappear, as he puts it, 'like snow off a dyke.' The nature of the work had changed drastically.

Now he feared for the 'good club life' of Church House. 'There were many youngsters who needed the club and what it could offer them—they would get it nowhere else in Bridgeton—and they also deserved our concern. I could guess what would happen to Church House under Geoff's ministry but I could not, and did not want to, deny his concern for some of the worst disadvantaged in the parish.'

Shaw threw himself into the work at Church House and became a popular and respected leader, always available, endlessly patient with the tough guy and outsider. As Ron Ferguson recounts in his biography, *Geoff!*, when criticised for the time he spent with delinquents, he would reply, 'You can't get lower than the cross.'

Ferguson also describes how Shaw would meditate on the idea of the abundant life which Jesus spoke of. 'What was there in life for youngsters from broken homes, brought up in slums, dealt with harshly by the police, institutionalised, robbed of prospects? He felt that such crippled young people needed the compensation of extra care and time and the opportunities of widened horizons.'

Geoff Shaw embraced that belief with a passion that excited both admiration and exasperation in his colleagues. The assistant minister at St Francis, Bill Shackleton, soon to play his own leading role in Church House, recalled in an article that Shaw intended to write a book about their boys entitled *Angels Unawares*. Shackleton comments wryly: 'Amongst those who were unaware that our charges were angelic, I had always stood in the foremost rank, regarding Geoff's penchant for seeing his geese as swans as a result of some kind of vitamin deficiency in his diet.'

John Sim describes Shaw as 'a driven man with a burden on his shoulders, sometimes it was a cross and sometimes it seemed a guilt-ridden class consciousness; but withal, a charismatic figure and the stuff of which saints are made.' Sim watched Church House change under Shaw's leadership. Inevitably, as he had foreseen, the balance shifted towards the tough guys.

'He did for Church House what I had feared. It was never the same again. No club can serve two masters. No matter what the leaders attempt, the members will decide.'

Shaw left Church House in 1957, to launch himself into the Gorbals experiment which had at last been given the go-ahead. He had given much to Bridgeton and gained much from it. In a way, says Sim, it formed his future, a future which would one day encompass the convenorship of the giant Strathclyde Regional Council.

Although Geoff Shaw's two years at Boden Street had proved a watershed, the club found a happy equilibrium under his successor. Big George Buchanan-Smith, son of Lord Balerno and assistant minister at Glasgow Cathedral, moved into Shaw's single-end in London Road and took over the boys' leadership for the next four years.

Built like a rugby forward, Buchanan-Smith was more of a team-worker than Shaw and, says Sim, 'by his own hearty methods restored something of what had been lost without losing much of what had been gained.' He, too, gave himself wholly to Bridgeton and ultimately suffered in health with a lengthy bout of hepatitis.

By the end of the fifties, Church House was ready to face a new chapter. John Sim had not had an easy furrow to plough. From the day he arrived, money problems loomed large. The tailing-off of the post-war interest in clubs and the tightening of belts at the Home Board meant that salaries and running costs could never be taken for granted; the struggle to pay bills was endless. Certainly, it was no sinecure at Church House and St Francis.

But Sim had kept Arthur Gray's vision burning bright. He had ridden the crises of finance and leadership at Church House, while building up St Francis at a time when other churches in the area were folding. He was utterly dedicated to cherishing the special ethos that incorporated both church and club. One of the most telling tributes to his success came, quite casually one day, from the janitor of Queen Mary Street School, who remarked to him in surprise, 'I see you've got the corner boys in your kirk.'

Always, members of Church House were crossing the bridge between Boden Street and Queen Mary Street. Throughout its history the club has been seen as the vestibule of the Church and all the ministers of St Francis have worked tirelessly to encourage maturing members 'to push open the door into the sanctuary,' as John Sim puts it. 'That there were always some who did this was a joy and a satisfaction, but serving the youngsters in the club was also an end in itself.'

Early in 1960, Sim decided to follow his predecessors at St Francis up the east coast, in his case as far as Kirkcaldy. Geoff Shaw was invited to succeed him, but turned the job down. George Buchanan-Smith was also asked, but he felt by then that his time in Bridgeton was coming to a natural close. One man did feel the job was for him, though, and spent many an anxious week awaiting the call.

Rev William Shackleton (Bill Shackleton, as he was known to all) had spent three years as assistant minister at St Francis, holed up in the little caretaker's flat in Church House. He then stayed on in Bridgeton as a kind of 'worker-priest', continuing to live in his tiny cell while taking on temporary teaching jobs and helping at the club in his spare time. He had a feeling that one day his relationship with the place would become more permanent.

Sure enough, in the autumn of 1960, he was inducted to St Francis-in-the-East and, with it, inherited both the chairmanship of Church House and some of the most difficult years in its history. The '60s were at hand, the people of Bridgeton were being decanted and the vandals were learning their trade. Church House would have a greater struggle than ever to survive. It was all on Bill Shackleton's shoulders.

REV
WILLIAM SHACKLETON

Survival

IF Sydney Warnes was the extrovert, Arthur Gray the saint and John Sim the organiser, Bill Shackleton was *par excellence* the survivor: a stubborn man, an enthusiast who could be funny and witty, but was not always the most diplomatic or patient of travellers in the bureaucratic byways that Church House was having to tread more and more frequently in the search for funding. He describes himself in those years as 'the man's man cum bloody-minded anti-establishment figure who was going to see all that St Francis-in-the-East stood for survived at any cost.'

Bill Shackleton fitted the place like a glove. He always felt this was his natural habitat and he stayed a further twenty-three years. Since leaving, his busy pen has produced a steady stream of articles and reminiscences about the place in typically exuberant, sardonic and self-deprecating style. These sometimes underplay the strain and the pain of the work at Bridgeton, but are un-matched for graphic detail.

In a prize-winning article for *The Scots Magazine*, he recalled the sincere, bespectacled figure he first cut in Bridgeton, fresh out of theological college, fluent in Greek and Hebrew:

'I stood under the Umbrella at Bridgeton Cross, and sensed something had been lacking in my training. I met few Hebrew speakers in the Cactus Bar; and nothing had been done to prepare me for refereeing a football match on the bloody fields of Glasgow Green.

'I knew a lot about peace and justice being a good thing; and had a soft spot for the love-ins and work-ins which were such fun in those days. The trouble was I had had little experience of break-ins, which formed such a popular recreational feature of Church House.

'Thankfully, I was quickly hit over the head with a chair at a club dance, and the scales fell from my eyes.'

By the time he took over as chairman of Church House, Shackleton had few illusions left, and soon knew more about mending roofs than a qualified slater. The roof was a favourite means of illegal entry in the sixties.

He was greatly helped in the early years by the towering leadership of John Webster, who took over as warden from George Buchanan-Smith. While still a probationer minister in Wellington Church in Glasgow's West End (a universe away from Bridgeton), Webster had heard a talk by Buchanan-Smith and accepted his invitation to visit.

'I well remember going up this dark, narrow lane,' he recalls today, 'the club on one side, the tenements of London Road on the other, midgey bins {refuse buckets} overturned at the top of the lane where the entrance was. No bell. Knocking wasn't heard. I was later to learn that entry was gained by kicking the metal-plated bottom of the door until the guy with the keys opened up.

'Inside it was dingy, sweaty, dirty, noisy and alive. One felt vulnerable—the defences of the pulpit, the study, the dog-collar, were no use here. How to make contact? I was, frankly, from a different social milieu. It was easy to say hello to the club leaders, but what to say to the members, the youngsters for whom the club existed? "Are you working?" "Naw." "That's tough." "Aye." '

Despite his feelings of inadequacy, John Webster knew as he walked away that night that he would be back. A few weeks later, he was invited to apply for Buchanan-Smith's job as boys' leader, and in the late summer of 1960 he and his new wife, Jennifer, moved into the warden's residence at 983, London Road.

It was all a bit different from Wellington. Their room and kitchen enjoyed the use of a stairhead cludgie (toilet) complete with a little battery-operated light. The wash-house for both clothes and body was three minutes round the corner, and the woodworm riddling a cupboard door turned out to be where a dart-board had hung. They soon grew used to the alarm call of the first trams rattling outside their bedroom window on the first run to Auchenshuggle at six in the morning.

They were warmly welcomed by Bridgeton neighbours and the folk of St Francis and, as John Webster came to know the community and the youngsters of the club, he felt that the Church was at last in touch with people in a real way. 'No longer was one passing by on the other side, as were the cars heading south on business or on holiday along London Road.'

He threw himself into the life of the club, soon swept up in the multifarious duties of the leader, which included helping youngsters to find work, appearing in court on behalf of others and supervising football from dawn to dusk on a Saturday. Weekday evenings were spent at the club, often stuck 'on the door'—locking, unlocking and negotiating terms of entry. A graded nightly sub was levied and led to exchanges such as: 'Gonna let me in, John? Ah'm skint this week.' 'Sorry, Jimmy.' Followed by, 'Hector, gonna lend me a tanner—the big yin'll no' let me in.'

From time to time, the ultimate sanction would be imposed and persistent miscreants barred, the reaction of the excluded offender often revealing just how much the club did matter to him after all. 'You were told what to do with one's .... awful club, and to add force to the message, the door would be kicked followed, on occasion, by a brick being hurled,' says Webster.

He particularly remembers a lad called Shug, who, on being told he was out, picked up a large table, ripped the legs off and threw them across the hall, before departing into the night.

'It was "night" indeed for Shug,' Webster recalls. 'He had an asthmatic father who sat by the fire all day, and a mother who tried her best, but when finding Shug with a knife proudly told me she had taken it from him and hidden it down the side of the chair. Poor Shug was later to find his brother, dead, hanging from the stairhead toilet cistern chain.

'We had Shug on TV once in connection with the club. The interviewer asked him what he liked best about the club. "S'easy—ra fitba," says Shug. "And anything you don't like, Shug?" "Aye, s'easy tae—they prayers!"

'And yet one can remember Shug in the club chapel looking wide-eyed, longing—it seemed—to be fed, needing to discover what his miserable life was all about.

'RA FITBA'

33

'To those who have known it, at least to some extent, love is a marvellous concept and they hunger for more. To those who have not known it, those who have been deprived of their birthright to be wanted, loved and given significance, then all attempts to make such a gift are viewed with great distrust.

'And yet the club existed to show that someone, the Church, did care, that someone did want those insecure offenders. The club persisted in believing in their worth and strove to enable them to enter life with confidence and to walk the earth with dignity.'

John Webster, with his big heart and his happy-go-lucky personality, was dreadfully missed when he left the club, after four years, to become a missionary in India.

After his departure, the perennial headache of finding full time staff of the calibre to cope with the challenges of Church House became a nightmare. There followed years of stop-gap leadership. Excellent people with formidable gifts would help out for a few months at a time, using it as a period of training for the ministry or the diaconate. But there was no stability, no continuity.

Looking back today, Bill Shackleton comments bleakly: 'The club went down and down in the sixties.'

Part of the trouble was that, despite the firm, down-to-earth leadership of men like George Buchanan-Smith and John Webster, the trend towards the delinquent at Church House had continued. Perhaps it was inevitable, in view of what was happening to Bridgeton as a community. It was being ravaged.

People were being moved out to the new housing schemes springing up all over Glasgow. They went hopefully; it seemed a blissful prospect at the time to exchange a single end in London Road for a new house with three bedrooms in Castlemilk, Easterhouse or Cumbernauld.

Back in Bridgeton, the slum tenements were coming down and eventually the new housing would appear—high blocks and uniform boxes, but better than the slums. But it all took so long. In the years between the scattering of the old community and building the shell of a new one, the place was laid waste.

In 1968, Bill Shackleton described the situation in a report to the Home Board:

'Redevelopment seems as far off as ever. In terms of human life, the cost is plain to see in poor health, a leaderless community, in juvenile delinquency so well advertised on every wall. It is easy to avoid the realities of such places in Glasgow today, either by ignoring their existence or becoming conditioned to them.

'Recent years have inexorably driven Church House away from being a community centre dealing with all ages. Adults no longer wish to come to a building showing all the signs of occupation by youngsters of the locality. So the club has become exclusively a youth club, and because parents of more respectable families are afraid to let their youngsters attend, it is a club for the poorer families.'

That report spoke, too, of the endemic financial problems of Church House:

'The work of the past year has been shadowed by the extensive damage done by thieves who stripped lead from the roof and caused water damage, mainly in the form of dry-rot. Existing through donations, corporation grants and the support of the Home Board, the resources of the club have been sorely drained by the repairs.'

Like his predecessor, Bill Shackleton soon got used to living in precarious financial waters. One year, there was a church balance at St Francis of precisely £2 and the Shackleton phone had to be cut off on occasions. But the church continued self-supporting—no mean feat—and Church House somehow kept going.

Shackleton calls its survival through those times 'a miracle'. Others might be more inclined to suggest that what saved Church House was in fact the man himself, with his enthusiastic belief in the place and the faith it was there to proclaim, his unshakable determination that it would not fail.

But it was a close thing. By the late sixties, the old Bridgeton was gone, the industry was gone, many of those very families who had been the backbone of the church and the club had gone. You could look out from Church House across the streets that divided it from St Francis, and there was nothing. No houses, no factories, no people. It was hard not to wonder if it was perhaps time to close the doors and move on with the tide.

'By 1969,' says Bill Shackleton, 'without full-time staff, broke, the building riddled with damp and rot, I faced the end I had long striven to avoid.'

Perhaps, then, it *is* a miracle that of all the churches in the Bridgeton area—and there were still some eight or nine Church of Scotland charges there in John Sim's time, St Francis alone has survived, and Church House is serving that still blighted patch of Glasgow with more gusto and Christ-centred commitment than ever before.

One spark of hope was enough for Bill Shackleton to seize upon. That August, harried by a plague of bluebottles and a dead rat in the cellar, he finally

Shackleton told the congregation of St Francis that he would be disappearing into the club for a year, emerging only for Sunday services. Twelve months later, Church House was a flourishing concern again.

He could scarcely have realised it at the time, but, in young Alex Mair, Shackleton had found the kind of man that Church House had long needed, a youth leader prepared to offer it the long term commitment that alone could give the work there stability. The St Francis ministers had always given it their wholehearted support, often driving themselves to ill-health trying to hold the place together while maintaining a busy church and parish. But it had never had a leader, working alongside the minister, who identified this as his life's work and stayed.

Alex Mair was the man. He had lived and breathed the club since he was six years old, when his next-door-neighbour in London Road, John Milligan, ushered him along to Church House one evening. Milligan was a stalwart elder in St Francis and a voluntary leader at the club, one of that battalion of heroes who must await a fuller history to enjoy the credit due to them, but who have always been the very backbone of the place. Every

acknowledged defeat. Sitting in the minute St Francis vestry, he despaired of Church House. At that very moment there was a knock on the door and a young lawyer from Cardonald called Tony Ireland popped his head round. Could he possibly help as a voluntary leader?

'Thus,' says Shackleton, 'did the good Lord save his servant's bacon.' His despair lifted further when he met one of his old junior boys from the club, a chap called Alex Mair, and asked him to lend a hand too. Then kind of person from unemployed folk to the managing director of a firm, from local grannies to a retired director of education, have done their bit down the years.

To John Milligan belongs the particular credit of introducing to Church House the boy who would define its future. Young Alex had a whale of a time there. To a six-year-old it was an overwhelming place at first, huge and cavernous. But once inside, clutching your two big copper pennies, no-one ever wanted to leave. He and his pals had to be regularly ejected at closing time from up the steeples and winkled out from all the fascinating nooks and crannies.

As he grew into adolescence, Mair came under the Christian influence of the club leaders. Indeed, he is one of the finest examples you could look for of the success of Church House in precisely the terms that its founder dreamed of. For Alex Mair, who came from a loving family but one without church connections, the club was a missionary post in the heart of the community, a bridge into the Church and the whole realm of Christian faith. Club membership led to Sunday School and on to an awareness that Christ was what mattered in his life.

'It's something that grows in you,' he says today. 'There's an old saying in Bridgeton that it's better felt than telt. That's how it was with me and that's how I try to pass it on.'

As he reached the end of his teens, Mair began to feel that his vocation was for missionary work abroad. He had been deeply influenced by John Webster, who had now left Church House for India. With all his youthful zeal, Alex felt India must be the place for him, too. Then, suddenly, he had a revelation. It loomed up one night in the club in the unlikely shape of Bill Shackleton.

Shackleton, at that time in 1968 hungry for full time help, asked him out of the blue if he would like to become leader himself. In fact, on receiving a glimmer of interest, what Shackleton actually did in his blunt way was to hand him the keys and suggest he leave his job (a very secure one as a turner in the local bowls factory) immediately.

It did not take Mair long to realise that here, on his very doorstep, was where the missionary call was pulling him. 'Suddenly,' he says, 'you wake up one day and the work that you've been participating in takes on a new form. It was a great revelation for me to sense that the work had to be done here.'

As the formal prelude to his appointment, he had to go before the club's management committee. He remembers simply feeling compelled to say he would take the job on. He needed no reminders that the place was falling apart, in more ways than one. The room they met in, dubbed—with the self-mocking irony that has always typified the place—'the executive room', was entirely derelict. One of the management committee said to him, 'Well, Mr Mair, what interests you in a place like Church House?'

'Immediately behind his head,' says Alex Mair, 'was this huge hole in the wall, which must have been about five feet in diameter, and I laughed at myself. I suppose he had a point. But I just felt that God was calling me.

'The motto of the club was "Rise up and Build", and I had always associated that with the fabric of the place. Every Saturday afternoon we'd meet here and set about repairing the break-ins that had occurred in the week and replacing the slates. And that of course was a practical experience of rising up and building. But I began to see that it was more than just the fabric. The lives needed just as much rebuilding. It was through that learning process that the Christian faith to me became a real, living thing.'

All the same, his first official years in Boden Street were testing ones for that faith. He and Bill Shackleton worked seemingly endless hours of the day and night to keep the witness of Church House alive into the seventies, in the teeth of break-ins, dry-rot and chronic under-funding. Many a time they would sit there on dark winter nights with no roof and the snow coming in, just to sustain that vital contact with the community, as Arthur Gray and his disciples had done in the early days. They even had to strip the bare walls of the old library for firewood to keep warm.

In Mair's first year, there was not even the guarantee of a salary. Four days before Christmas he had scarcely a penny to his name and insidious thoughts were beginning to surface, like: 'This Christianity's OK, but it's a different story when it hits your pocket, when you can't pay the bills.'

Then what he likes to think of as the Providence which has always cherished Church House through the bad times, intervened. He opened a Christmas card and out fluttered a cheque for £50. 'It was almost,' he says, 'as if Providence was saying, "Well, don't look back now".'

Providence had a busy time of it in those years. The guardians of Church House once had a gas bill for £1,300, following a gas leak that had never been traced. When they couldn't pay, they got a letter to say the gas

would be cut off. That same morning, they received a donation of £1,000, and two days later came word that an old lady had died and left £300 to Church House in her will.

Church House has always lived like that, and as Arthur Gray used to say, 'We've never starved a winter yet', although it can be a terrible strain. But the doors would not have been open for long without the support of the Church of Scotland and the local authorities. It has never been quite enough, never without its headaches, but the debt over fifty years is incalculable.

It was thanks to the Kirk's Home Board (nowadays called the Board of National Mission) and to grants from the Scottish Education Department that extensive rebuilding was at last undertaken in the early '70s. Dryrot always concentrates the mind, and its discovery meant a new ultimatum—either close or rebuild. Shackleton, the survivor, opted to have a go. He was told it would cost £27,000, but the final cost was nearly four times as much and he was still paying it off several years after the place re-opened in 1974.

Perhaps only Arthur Gray with his own soul-wearying experience of the hassles and disappointments and time-consuming negotiations of trying to produce the original Church House, could have understood what a struggle it was to rebuild it. Indeed, if Shackleton had known the final cost, he would never have started in the first place. Today, he is uncharacteristically short-winded about the experience: 'It made me a good deal less naive than I had been.'

But at least by 1974 they at last had a purpose-built club, clean and water-tight, with facilities for the girls, hard-wearing play areas outside and an air of solid indestructibility. The S.E.D. had been, in Shackleton's own words, 'splendid', and let him design the whole place exactly as he wanted it. That meant doors opening outwards so that they couldn't be kicked in, no windows and all pipes well buried. He knew his clientele.

He was especially pleased with the addition of a separate area upstairs to which the girls could retreat. The Martha and Mary room, with oven and sink and books and paints, became a focus for the less obstreperous activities of the club. Here you could bake and sew, practise hairdressing, create a work of art or just lounge around with a magazine.

Instead of the big chapel, where the presence of eighty wise-cracking teenagers with their mouths full of chips had turned the epilogue into something of an ordeal, there was now the Upper Room—smaller, more intimate, more inviting. It was dedicated to the memory of Arthur Gray.

Alex Mair, who had once had to fetch a ten-foot long pole from the sawmill to control the back-row revellers in the old chapel, found that the youngsters now queued up to savour the mysteries of the Upper Room.

'It's funny,' he says, 'Because there are doors on the Upper Room and I say to them, "No, you're not getting in there, you're not old enough", they're all wanting in. So I say, "OK, we'll go in tomorrow night", and they can hardly wait.

'Then we open up and put the lights on and they all sit there quite the thing and we start talking. I might say, "Why do you think this place is here? What's that cross on the wall?" Very simple things. It's amazing how kids pick things up and say, "Oh, that's Jesus. Jesus hung on the cross, didn't he?" And I say, "Aye, that's right. Why do you think that happened?" It's a very simple, elemental development until they all come to an understanding.'

Mair and Shackleton continued their partnership right through the seventies, the one in charge of the day-to-day running of the club, the other up to his neck in

'RA FITBA' IN THE 'SEVENTIES

bureaucratic tangles in the search for money to keep the place going, while grappling with the demands of a busy parish.

Their main funding came in the form of a grant from Strathclyde Region. For a long time, this was used to pay all the bills and what was left formed Mair's

41

wages. Then they found there was money available for salaries from Government regeneration grants, which put his own on a more regular footing and enabled them to hire a girls' leader to work alongside him.

It all held together for a while, but then there came a clash of policy. East End regeneration was the buzzword of the times and Bridgeton was awash with public money. New houses, new jobs, new community, a new future: that was the dream, and the people of Church House who had kept a single flame of hope alive in Bridgeton long before it was fashionable, were all for it. But they insisted on one thing: the *raison d'être* of their club was Christian witness, it was specifically committed to making the Gospel relevant in the area. That commitment must remain.

This was not, however, a policy that went down well with the group of Community Education councillors who currently held the purse-strings and whose vision of Bridgeton's future was determinedly secular. Mair and Shackleton were grilled repeatedly over their finances and the ethos of Church House.

'In the end,' says Mair, 'we told them just to keep the grant, because we had our policy and the local authorities had theirs. They thought that if they could stop the

salaries coming here, the place would close down and they could use the money for their own youth work.' This they eventually did, but Church House is still the pre-eminent provision for the young people of the area, now surviving without any assistance from national or local government sources.

It would be strange, in a way, if there had not been times of tension between the purse-holders and the club, with its habit of prickly independence instilled over years of having to fight its corner at every turn. But the strain of it all made Bill Shackleton's last years at St Francis and Church House less happy than they might have been and, when he was unexpectedly invited to take over a church in Greenock in 1983, he accepted.

Shackleton departed exhausted. But he left Church House intact, its fabric secure and its commitment to the Gospel undiminished. To it, and to the wider parish, he had given everything in those twenty-three years (twenty-eight, if you count the years as assistant), as had his wife Margaret. Like all the St Francis wives—and Kathy Mair today—she had made many untold sacrifices of family life and husband's company to keep the light shining in Bridgeton. (Indeed, Sydney Warnes' long-suffering wife is said to have hated the place and expressed a close interest in putting a bomb in St Francis.)

Among the piles of typewritten reports in the Church House files, Shackleton left one of the most lucid statements of the conviction that had guided him and his predecessors along the often bumpy Boden Street journey:

'We have found that, through the agency of Church House, the local church has been put into a living relationship with its parish. Our work is to maintain that relationship at all costs.

'It means fulfilling our total ministry in terms of the place in which God has set us as servants. It means listening before proclaiming. It means striving to make the faith visible, desirable and recognisable. But the greatest guiding conviction of all is simply this—that it works. God continues to give the kind of success He wants from our miserable endeavours ....

'The important thing is to love humanity and to remember that, as James Joyce once put it, God is a shout in the street.'

Perhaps it is because men like Bill Shackleton, John Sim, Arthur Gray and Sydney Warnes (and the present incumbent of St Francis, the Rev Howard Hudson) held unshakably to these principles, through thick and thin, that Church House is flourishing to this day, an example—if a tough one to follow—for any church which wants to reach the unreachable in its midst.

What Bill Shackleton also left behind at Church House was a committed leader—another man who believed in those same ideals and had the determination to carry them through the eighties and beyond.

The mantle passed to Alex Mair.

Still Shouting in the Street

ALEX Mair's salary had never been what you might call secure. It came and it went, and when the funding stopped he watched it retreat again with a certain resignation. The girls' leader, Margaret Beaton, was in the same position. They decided to carry on unemployed, in the belief that they were doing the work God wanted them to.

That was when the Church of Scotland stepped in and shouldered another load of the responsibility it had first accepted all those years ago. The Home Board offered to train them, and pay them, as deacon and deaconess, lay missionaries in Bridgeton. (Alex Mair saw the word 'pension' attached to his name for the first time since he was handed the keys to Church House.) Running costs remained dependent on a grant from Strathclyde Region (see p 41) and on indispensable but fitful donations from private individuals, churches and faithful Glasgow trusts.

Alex Mair and Margaret Beaton each had twelve months' training at St Colm's in Edinburgh, one at a time

44

so that there was always someone to hold the fort back home. When both had returned, they formed a team ministry in the parish with the new minister, Howard Hudson, who has since been able to do what none of his predecessors had the luxury of doing—concentrate on the church while the club flourishes under stable, independent leadership.

Margaret Beaton has proved another of the great 'finds' of Church House. A local girl who had tasted the fun and been influenced by the fellowship of Church House as a youngster, she became more and more involved in her teens. When the urban aid grant enabled the club to employ a girls' leader, she had no hesitation in giving up her job at Templeton's carpet factory. She had received so much from the club; it was time to give something back.

Her remit is as wide as Mair's is—from visiting local schools, to teaching baking and sewing in the Martha and Mary room, to presiding over a hot bath when it's needed. Alex Mair has an enlightening story about the kind of impact she has been quietly making on the lives of families in the area.

'About twelve years ago, a chap came to visit here, an ex-military policeman who looked every inch the part. He had black leather gloves that were so highly polished you could see your face in them. His shoes were gleaming and he had this big, black crombie.

'He had a calling to the ministry and he used to sit at the door for us, collecting the subs. One night he noticed that some kids were coming in black and filthy and going home clean. I explained that some families were neglected and Margaret gave them a shower and a spray and a change of clothing and some soup.

'He said he would like to visit this family. So we went round and I showed him. And there was this family—mother had run away to London, father was an alcoholic, and they were squatting in the London Road in a tenement building.

'And do you know, there wasn't any door, it was just a bit of cloth that covered the front entrance. There was no electricity, there was an up-turned midden bin in the corner with a candle on it and a dirty, stinking mattress in the corner, and that's what they were sleeping on.

'For these kids, Church House was their home, we were their family, because Margaret cleaned them, clothed them, fed them, and they came back the next night. Now one of them is married and her kids come here.'

Today, in 1991, there are not so many abandoned children in squalid squats. Neglect tends to take more insidious forms. The great commodity that Church House offers the youngsters of the neighbourhood these days is *time*.

'It's amazing,' says Mair. 'Some houses that you go into in the area are visually poverty-stricken, and yet the kid will have a video recorder and a ghetto-blaster and a colour television. And faither's lying drunk in the corner and there's no carpet on the floor. They talk about the Third World—it's not so very far away in some senses.'

Margaret Beaton used to wonder why baking and simple crafts were so popular with the children. 'Then it dawned on me that some youngsters are so used to having things like videos and computers, that they go into their rooms and shut the door. Whereas the club is going back to basics and offering them what they don't have—relationships, sharing.'

Bridgeton today has an official label: 'multi-deprived'. Unemployment is high. The post-regeneration wilderness is a monument to wasted dreams. Factories that were thrown up in the enthusiasm of the GEAR project are largely demolished, the rubble still lying about, the vermin creeping. Those industrial units that have survived employ a handful of people at most.

The housing is better than the old days, if you can stand living alone in the sky. But there is little sense of community these days. Now that the money is done and the agencies gone, Bridgeton feels forgotten once more. And at Church House they are counting the human cost, as usual.

'No matter how much we may try to hide it and retain a bit of pride and say to people, "There's a world here to improve", we're battling against all the odds,' says Alex Mair.

'Now drug pushers are coming into the area selling hard drugs. Children much younger than 12 are thinking like 19-year-olds. They're coming under the influence of the pushers very young, which is why it's so essential that we have a presence here.'

But he and Margaret Beaton have never regarded their youthful charges as 'problems'. They resist categorising and analysing, they are refreshingly free of jargon. Ask about the kind of children who come and Mair hesitates:

'Yes, there's alcohol abuse. Yes, there's drug abuse. Yes, there's a criminal element. There's gambling as young as five or six. All the problems are here. But we don't want to generalise and label people into categories.

'What we try to do here is to open the doors and, yes, the people with the problems come. But they're not made to feel that they've got problems, although we're very aware of what they are, and we work in our own fashion at getting alongside and doing what we can.

'At the end of the day, we're simply adopted mothers and faithers, the voluntary leaders that come here are aunties and uncles. It's a home for kids in the area, whether they're good or bad, better off or not. We try to accommodate all these different aspects of life in the community.'

In a sense, the club has outlived the shifts of emphasis with which it responded to the varying needs of previous decades, and returned to the all-embracing function of its earliest days. No longer merely the last place of refuge for the delinquent, it is genuinely a home for all, from the three or four-year-olds tagging after their siblings, to the pensioners who come for their lunch and take off every summer in a bus to Lindisfarne for a week.

The emphasis now is on targeting the schools and

ALEX MAIR AND THE KIDS AT LINDISFARNE

offering the world-weary ten-year-olds of the nineties an alternative to the temptations of the street corners. Trips to the country in summer, holidays on Lindisfarne, winter games, a chance to tear around or the opportunity to be quiet and create something, an invitation to the Upper Room to learn about Jesus: half a century on, it's much as Arthur Gray dreamed it would be. A house, a home, a place where young people are given time.

And the faith of the place burns as steady as those first candles on the joiner's bench. It's a no-nonsense spirituality, the Gospel Bridgeton-style.

'One evening,' says Mair, 'there was a group of tots in, five or six-year-olds, and some of them were gambling. One of them, he's not even at school yet, came up to me in the canteen, his trousers away round his knees and no socks on, and he was filthy. And he pulled out this dod of plasticine, all full of feathers and dirt.

'I was in the course of talking to him about Jesus, so I started making these figures for him with the plasticine. I made a wee cross and I went through the whole process of Jesus being put on trial and being put on the cross, and the sleeve of my jaicket was a cave. By this time, there must have been about eight of them around us, and they were so enthralled.

'The next night when he comes in, he's only two minutes inside the door when he says, "Alec, are we going up to see Jesus the night?"'

The leaders need all the ingenuity they can muster at Church House. They always have. For a while, they tried holding the Sunday School on a Friday, because the building was packed that night. First attempts to interest eighty rowdy clients in Bible stories and choruses resulted in predictable bedlam. So the leaders upturned the goalposts in the gym and put a plank of wood across and wellington boots on top. Then they produced an old tennis ball.

'Right,' says Alex, 'we'll listen to the Bible story and we'll ask some questions and those that are listening, if you get the right answer, you get three shots at knocking these things down.'

The Bible Club, as the youngsters named it themselves, proved a roaring success.

It can be tiring, draining work. But the Upper Room is always there, and when the children clatter out—over a hundred of them some nights—that is where the leaders take time to be quiet and remind themselves of why they are there and what it means to serve.

'Why, at the end of the day, do we carry on?' says Alex Mair. 'I've always seen it as a labour of love in its proper sense, and that is steeped in faith. These are really the two elements that drive me—I just love what I'm doing here, and have a deep faith that it's right and we're not alone.

'I'm very conscious of that. Humanly and physi-cally, you sometimes feel alone. But this place has survived against all the odds. It should have been dead and buried. It's survived on faith.'

His hope for Church House in the future is much like Arthur Gray's: that the club will remain a source of stability and security in the area for its youngsters, that it will continue to provide a surrogate family life rooted in unchanging values but with the courage—and the means—to adapt to new times.

Its survival depends on faith, yes; on Providence, always; but on human agencies too. It depends on volunteers continuing to give their time. It depends on local authorities recognising the value of the work. And it depends, crucially, on the ongoing loyalty of the Church of Scotland and its members.

It was a huge boost to the morale of Church House when the Woman's Guild chose the club as the recipient of its fund-raising in 1991-92. If enough is raised, the funds will be used to replace the old canteen with a modern soda parlour, re-equip the play area for the youngest children and generally update the place. It needs it.

For fifty years, God's people at Church House have obeyed the call to rise up and build. No-one will ever know how many broken lives they have helped rebuild.

Now it is the turn of the tatty old walls, the second-hand equipment and the bolted-down tables to have their day. It is a chance to offer the youngsters of Bridgeton not just a place of their own, but an attractive place of their own, fortifications and all.

Margaret Beaton puts it this way: 'We've always worked on a shoe-string, it's always been second-best in material terms. What we have now in the nineties is the chance, for once, to offer the kids the best.

'Once they're here we can offer them the best again—a real, live faith that works. And then let them make the decision with careful nurture—and a wee push now and again from the people in here.'

Arthur Gray could hardly have put it better.

If you would like to send a donation
or become a 'Friend of Church House',
please write to
ALEX MAIR
at
BRIDGETON,
ST FRANCIS-IN-THE-EAST CHURCH HOUSE,
6 Boden Street, Glasgow G40 3PU.